The Alpha, the Omega, My KING

A Walk With Jesus Through Poetry

By Catherine P. Larsen

RoseDog Books
PITTSBURGH, PENNSYLVANIA 15238

The contents of this work including, but not limited to, the accuracy of events, people, and places depicted; opinions expressed; permission to use previously published materials included; and any advice given or actions advocated are solely the responsibility of the author, who assumes all liability for said work and indemnifies the publisher against any claims stemming from publication of the work.

All Rights Reserved
Copyright © 2023 by Catherine P. Larsen

No part of this book may be reproduced or transmitted, downloaded, distributed, reverse engineered, or stored in or introduced into any information storage and retrieval system, in any form or by any means, including photocopying and recording, whether electronic or mechanical, now known or hereinafter invented without permission in writing from the publisher.

RoseDog Books
585 Alpha Drive, Suite 103
Pittsburgh, PA 15238
Visit our website at www.rosedogbookstore.com

ISBN: 979-8-88812-305-8
eISBN: 979-8-88812-805-3

The
Alpha,
the
Omega,
My
KING

A Walk With Jesus Through Poetry

Acknowledgments

To my Husband Brad,
who's music has filled my life with
melodies of love, kindness and passion.

And to my daughter Britney and her Husband Mike,
who taught me to believe in myself.

The Word

The Word encircles me as the planet
orbits the sun.
I too am encircled by the Son, with
one utter word, the universe began.
Your Holy Word encompassed the sphere
of time, space and eternity.
I am but a part of your Holy Word, a
miracle made out of the Breath of God,
which transforms all the beauty of the
universe in the pupil of an eye: which
sees the miraculous. The ear; which hears the
melodious. The hands; which touch the
mundane. And the heart, which leaps for
joy over the joy of the WORD.

The Incarnation

What made Him leave
      His heavenly place?
To take a servants place.
Could it have been
      me or you?
Impossible, you say,
well, it is true.

The Annunciation

Mary, knowing she was a lowly servant,
        was still aware
That, even though the Angel with
        majestic stare
Did not confuse the summons to become,
        mother of the Most High,
For she had known since birth, her lowliness did
        not keep her, from His side.
Though troubled with the thought of
        not knowing man,
She did not once decide not to take a stand.
The question that was given her on High, was
        given back by her "Yes", as her reply.
Now we can all be rest assured,
That the day when the Angel delivered
        his word,
That we also have a light that shines
        in us
The gift of rebirth from the Holy Spirit
        we can trust.
Who lives in each and everyone anew,
        to show us what the Lord can really do.
We too can become the epitome of
        sainthood like Mary.

The Visitation

Two brave and lovely Ladies
        are they both,
One carrying the child who's contained
        within the Host.
The other carrying the child who would
        declare His worth,
Of Mary's baby born of Godly birth.
Each woman as they greet eachother
Understand the meaning of their role as mother.
Elizabeth is content in knowing that
        her son is truly blessed,
To make the way for Mary's Son, who
        blesses those who are blessed.

The Birth of John the Baptist

He should be called John, the angel
    of the Lord declared,
For their was a labor of love
    prepared,
To herald in the dawn of day
Preparing us for the greatest day!
Our Lord our Master has come
    to dwell among us,
And dear St. John is the first
    to tell among us.

Joseph

Joseph must have felt confused,
at least to hear the very news,

That his betrothed is now conceived with child.
Not wanting to defile Mary's good name, questions compiled.

In a dream, Joseph was told Mary's condition,
Was an act of the Most High's mission,

To redeem the world with God's great Son.
He shall be called "Jesus", to save His people
          "He is the One".

The Nativity

I often wonder what it would be like
Without that Holy, tranquil night
When the greatest mediator, between
       us and God,
Was laid to rest in stable sod.
What would have happened without
       His grace,
Of sin being destroyed without
       a trace.
Where would we have gone for
       renewed strength?
With His merciful heart always at
       arms length.
What He has made possible, can not
       be undone,
With God the Most Holy and God's
       Holy Son.
He has given to us the greatest
       treasure,
His love from His heart which can
       never be measured!

The Shepard's

Shepherd's in hills and dales, tending their
        flocks by night.
Were terrified by a glorious sight.
The angel of the Lord said "Be not afraid, I
        bring you good news of great joy,
To you born today in the city of David, a
        Savior, the Messiah, the Lord, a boy.
The sign will be a child wrapped in a cloth
        lying in a manger".
Suddenly there was the angel, with a multitude of
        heavenly hosts, praising not as a stranger,
They were praising God and saying,
"Glory to God in the highest heaven and
on earth peace among those whom He favors!"

Three Wise Men

The three wise men traveling through the night,
Being guided by that magnificent star light

Were overcome with joy and awe
Of the lovely infant child they saw.

They knew at once they had found a King,
Yet, more royal than any king they knew.

They sensed He was destined to do great deeds,
And in Him found everything they would need.

A special warmth and love was felt,
As the three wise men tenderly knelt
Each one had a special gift to give,
Then they suddenly realized, that
He had come,
So they could abundantly live.
Jesus invites all to accept His
invitation.
He has been born for all creation
To let us live more abundantly.

The Presentation in the Temple

Jesus presented at the temple
with the offerings of a pair of doves,

Was declared by Simeon, with
so much love,

That he could announce this
miricale which came about,

He had seen our Savior, our Lord
Our Reedemer, without a doubt.

He could now rest in peace
at this heavenly best,

He now was assured of the
Word Made Flesh.

The Flight Into Egypt

The angel's word still ringing
in Joseph's ear,
Foretold how Herod's deed of fear,
To kill the child for want of
jealousy and pride.
Joseph at once packed up his
family to comply.
Safe in Egypt they can rest assure.
There is safety in His word.

The Return to Nazareth

Home to Nazareth at last
King Herod's ugly deeds have past

The Holy Family grows in grace,
Their will be no one to take their place.

For Jesus now is safe at last, though,
time will show what must come to pass.

Jesus Among the Doctors

He was in His Father's House
The place where all His longings
            were met.
All were amazed at His knowledge
            and yet,
His mother's question, why did He
            stay behind?
As she kneeled,
His place, His home, was
Now revealed.

John the Baptist

Clothed with camel hair, with a
leather belt around his waist,
The locust and wild honey
        he did taste.
He proclaimed "The One more powerful
        than I, is coming after me,
I am not worthy to stoop down and untie
        the sandals of His feet".
        Come see!

The Baptism of Jesus

You rising out of the water
have taken us within your heart-to
cleanse, the very portal to which
we become your children.

The Temptation of Jesus

For forty-days and forty-nights
The devil tempted Jesus with
    all his might.
Not once did He sucumb to the
    devils wishes,
For He had us in mind as
    the riches.

The Call of the Disciples

He knew at once who was to be
the rock of the church
        Come Follow Me!
He knew at once who would deny
        He rose.
Unless he touched His wounds.
He knew at once who would
        betray Him with a kiss,
Yet, He did not deviate from
        His list,
of the twelve, whom He loved.

Jesus Rejected at Nazareth

Aren't you the carpenters son?
Aren't you Mary's son?
How can you say "You are
        the One?'
Their unbelief kept all their
        longings unfulfilled,
For they, closing their eyes also
closed their hearts to the Son of Man,
who could have worked miracles
        in their midst.

The Wedding at Cana

Fill the jugs with
      water,
Was the order,
Only to find,
      The finest wine
was saved for last.

The Pool at Bethseda

The pools still water, not stirred
up for the ill man.

 "Would you like to be well?,
I can make you well. Pick
up your mat and walk".

The man amazed could barely talk.
Now his stirrings would be met interially.

The Man Brought in Through the Roof

In the lowering down
He was raised up
To a new level of purification.
Now being able to walk with
his head held high; because
of the sins that were forgiven him.

The Blind Man at Bethsaida

How important it is to see correctly in the
    Spiritual realm.
When Jesus used His own saliva, He
    bathed the eyes of the
    blind man, He took the helm,
And asked, "Can you see anything?"
To His reply, "I see people who look like trees."
Jesus laid His hands on his eyes again,
And he could see everything clearly.
    How important it is to see
    correctly in the Spiritual realm.

The Calming of the Storm

Fierce winds whipping up and down into the night.
The crew filled with uneasy fright.

Wake up dear Jesus or we shall die,
Oh, people of little faith it is "I",

Rebuking the wind, it now is calm.
The crew realizing, He has them in His palm.

He restored their inner peace,
And they know now, He restores, the very least.

The Gardinean Swine

The demons not relenting for
    their time.
        Asked Jesus for extra time,
            in being they wanted to be placed
                in the swine, and then
                    the swine rushed down the
                    steep incline,
                      and perished
out of time.

The Cure of the Nobleman's Son

A royal official whose son lay ill,
Was asked of Jesus to make him well.

Jesus was full of compassion and good will,
"Your son will live", was all He needed to tell.

The man believed, and started on his way.
His slave met him, told him his child would live.

The official knew their was no way to repay,
The gift of faith that Jesus did give.

Jaurius Daughter

Do not fear, she is not dead.
Give her something to eat,
For children need to be fed,
For the children of God
will not be left abandoned,
without heavenly bread.

The Hemorrhaging Woman

He felt her faith
With the touching of His hem.

He knew she would forever taste,
the benevolence of what was then.

The Multiplication of the Loaves

He multiplies everything that has meaning. To give as an abundance to what little we already have.

Jesus Walks on Water

I am not a stone,
I do not sink,
I am the One and
Only link.
To be your comforter
And your peace.
The storm will pass
For I command
The waves, the sea,
And all the land.

Peter Tries to Walk on Water

Is it You? Or a ghost?
If it is You, command me to
          come to You.
Come. For I am the Lord of Hosts.
Out went Peter,
in came fear.
Lord, save me!
I am here.
You of little faith,
why did you doubt?
I am the One who brings everything
          about.

The Transfiguration

Shall we stay and pitch
     a tent for three?
And maybe one for you and me?
I love the way I feel right now.
Can we stay forever
     in the cloud?
Jesus knew we must come down,
With heart and feet firmly
     on the ground.

The Man Born Blind

Rabbi, who sinned? The man or his parents?
That he was born blind.
Jesus said"Neither, since it was not
his time
Until now, he was born blind, so that
God's work might be revealed in him.
"As long as I am in the world I am
The Light of the world", said the man without sin.
When He said this, He spat on the ground
        and made mud.
Who could have immagined with so much
        love?
With the saliva He spread the mud
        on the man's eyes,
As He stood beside.
Go wash in the pool of Siloam.
He went, washed, came back, able to see,
        and then went home.

Two Blind Men

We are blind in
so many ways.

Turn our darkness into
bright rays.

Of love for the Master, who
heard our pleas,

And asked, "Do you believe?"
According to your faith, let it be done to you.

Our eyes were opened,
with a new purposeful view.

The Raising of Lazarus

Lazarus locked in the tomb
of death,
Could never have imagined
a second breath.
From the "Lord of Life" who
expressed His grief.
Called Lazarus from the tomb,
with great belief,
To resurrect Lazarus
from his sleep.
Lazarus came out,
bound head to toe.
Jesus said,
"Unbound him and let him go".

The Samaritan Woman at the Well

The well the water so deep and so clear
Was drawn up for the man who showed no fear
Of talking to a Samaritan woman about her condition
Of her life's history and rendition
She couldn't believe all the truth that was told
About her life's history was about to unfold
She had hidden like deep within the well
All of her treasures that were now drawn up
To tell, her thirst will now be satiated
By her new guest as she ran to tell all of the rest

Marie Magdalene

It was her intention to show her love
To the One who came from above.

Her incense was all she had to offer
Though, the other guests only thought of the coffer,

Of what she could have saved, instead of spent.
The action in God's heart, must have meant,

That all of her love, was poured out in that instance,
For her repentance and His forgiveness.

John the Baptist Beheaded

Around she danced
      for Herod's pleasure,
But in her heart, their
      was no treasure,
Of man's great worth and
      divine endowment
Of Christ's decree of John's
      announcement,
That he was one to speak
      the truth,
Of Christ supreme,
      and only proof.

Catherine P. Larsen

Mary and Martha

Martha asked Him in,
Mary took Him in.
Each one placed Him at
The head of their table.

Let the Children Come to Me

Children
Hidden in Him
Risen in Him
Intrinsically alive in Him
Safe in Him
Trustingly loving Him

Peter's Profession of Faith

I know you are the Son of God,
St. Peter would declare
          as a lightening rod.
No one before had spoken so plain
At the beauty of God's reign.
The keys of heaven shall
              prevail
Instead of Hades gates of
              hell.

You never completely close
          the door.
For You, the holder of the
          key,
Never completely departs
          from me!

Woman Following Jesus

God so loved woman that
He was born of woman

To share the greatness of His
Humanity to all, great and small.

The woman wanted to reside
And be by His side

As He walked the path of rightousness.

The Treasure Hidden in the Field

The treasure was there
     all along.
I just never realized
     my own worth,
Until Jesus revealed it
     to me.
Eternity.

The Mustard Seed

Though the mustard seed
      is little,
So was Jesus at
      His birth.
Yet, His message is
      not a riddle,
But, a compilation of
      His worth,
For the fruit of His
      crucifixtion,
Is the beginning of
      our birth.

The Good Samaritan

Could I be the one who walked
    on the other side
Of the street, who the Good
    Samaritan needed me not to hide
My unworthiness of not getting
    involved,
With my brother and all of
    his pitfalls?
He needed my help and
    my concern,
But, I did not turn.
I went straight ahead
Hoping my denial doesn't
shed,
any guilt.

The Lost Sheep

I am hoping the one lost
           is found.
For I know that it
won't be long until I
may lose my way, and need
a gentle hand to bring me
back to the fold where I
belong.

The Place of Honor

The nearer we are to God
The less we need to be seen
        by others.
By being God's, we learn
we are in the highest position
and cannot be brought
        low.

The Prodigal Son

I would like my inheritance
        was his stance,
The dear father gave him his wish
        with a loving glance.
He left his surroundings, no
        more would he roam
For he realized his needs
        could be met at home.
The father came running
        when he saw his son.
The son was so humbled
        as he did run,
Into his fathers arms,
        and declared with regret,
I shall work as a slave
        and never forget.
The father said, "My son, who
        was lost and now found"..
Their was shouting and
        laughter all around.
Put the ring on his finger
        and sandals on his feet.
My son will no longer
        wander the street.

The fated calf shall be killed
     and we shall all eat.
The other son was angry at all
     that was done
For the Prodigal son.
The loving father tried to explain
My love for you has never wained.
Your brother was dead and came
     back to life,
Instead of squabbling, jealousy, fear
     and strife.
Let us rejoice at his
     new life.

Bad and Good Seed

Let the word of God
  permeate me.
Let the will of God
  enfold in me.
Let not the evil doers
  sway me.
Let the love of God
  sustain me,
until the end of the world.

The Grain of Wheat

Dying you have raised
      me up
To new heights that I
      never imagined existed.
I have now become enlisted
In doing your holy work
Until you call me to
      yourself.
My greatest reward.

The Rich Man and Lazarus

Lazarus the long suffering
           servant
Knew that his time on earth
           was limited
and so, lived it out as fully
           as possible.
His heavenly home would be
           his reward,
For everything lacking, would
           be restored.

Catherine P. Larsen

The Laborers of the Vinyard

The Laborers in the field
Did not realize their yield

In working for Christ
All are compensated the same price,

Whether first or last.

Wedding Day

The Master is calling me,
        when I awake
Not for my own transforming
        sake.
He bids me to come as
        a loving bride
And to be aware of His
        enduring transforming side;
He asks not for deeds I
        could not fulfill,
Or a battle which is futile,
        conjured up by my will.
His eyes are upon me till dusk
        until dawn,
And "Blessed", He said,
For all of my children I
        enjoin to be wed.
For the grace of God is to
        be endowed
On the humble, compassionate,
        and less on the proud.
For you He calls to be His
        bride.
For all creation, He bids to

His side.
He has created, molded you
          of the palm of His hand,
For you too are important to His
          Salvivic Plan.
One thing is certain and can not
          be denied.
He has called us each by name
          to be His loving bride.

The Talents

He has given us talents of
       every kind,
Even the lame, the deaf
       and the blind.
Yet, most of us are unaware
       of our own great worth,
On how much the Lord compensated
       us at birth.
All He asks that we use our
       great skill,
To excell in the Spirit and
       not to stand still.

The Beatitudes

Eight times Christ blesses the people
of the beatitudes.
He could have only blessed them once,
but the emphasis shows how much
He loves:
> The poor in spirit
> Those that mourn
> The meek
> Those who thirst for righteousness
> The merciful
> The pure in heart
> The peacemakers
> Those who are persecuted for righteousness,

Those who revile you, and utter all kinds of evil against you
falsely
on my account.

Anger

I once was quiet, now I'm loud.
I once was peaceful, now I'm proud.
Anger has crept in some how.
Let me pray for repentance now.

When you Fast

In fasting I have found my
      way to you,
Like a precious new child
      fresh and new.
My life is not finished
      for you preserve,
The best part of me hidden
      in my reserve.

Knock and the Door Will be Opened

You are the light which shines through me,
You are the helper which makes me see,

That all above, below, beyond
Is but a gesture of your arm,

Outstreched to help along the way,
So I shall find my way each day.

You persevere when I am weak,
And tell me always to "Knock and Seek".

You give me guidance when I'm confused
And not to forsake Him if you loose.

For, He is with you till the end,
And forever you have found a friend.

Wolves in Sheep's Clothing

Those who devour, never truly enjoys the feast.

Who Are my Mother and my Brothers

You never once, dear Lord, gave me the impression that I am not as special as your loving Mother or your nearest relatives. You have made us "one" in your holy family, encompassing us in the very fabric of your life.

Take Up Your Cross

With the cross
We have no loss
Of how we must attain
The perfect actions of our aim
To be close to the
        "Savior".

Come To Me All Who Weary

Be still- my right hand will
      protect thee.
Be still- for you are the most
      precious to me.
Be still-for I will not leave
      you alone.
Be still- for I shall take
      you home.

Catherine P. Larsen

I Have Come To Cast Fire

I stroke the flame of
       love for you,
Do you not feel the touch
       of love?
Do you not hear the voice
       of love?
Do you not see the way
       of love?

The Needles Eye

Bloated by my own riches and feasting on this worlds glories, It will become harder to do the Saviors' bidding.

For now I am wrapped up in myself.

The Greatest Commandment

Without God we can not do anything, and without our neighbor we can not do anything for God.

The Stones Would Shout

If the stones could shout I believe this
is what they would say:

Shout out for God is good!
Shout out for God is love!
Shout out for God has
come down from above!
Shout out for Jesus has
taken our sins upon Himself!
He will die and rise
to save us from our sins!

Catherine P. Larsen

I Am Not Of This World

I am not of this world
It can not contain me.
For I am from above
And you are from below,
And I am here to bestow
The "Good News".

I Am The Good Shepard

To hear His voice and know
That He is calling me
Is to forever know what
I hope to see
The imprint of His heart
on mine,
Together beating forever
in time.

Catherine P. Larsen

The Last Judgment

When the last judgment comes to pass
I hope to be alas,
With the Lord, who has protected me
Throughout my path.

Separating The Sheep From The Goats

What can I say when He lays His hand
across my shoulder to separate me from the goats?
I pray He will find my repentance sufficient
enough to enter the fold with Him.

The Triumphal Entry Into Jerusalem

Look your King is coming mounted
on a colt a donkey,
He is humble and pure of heart,
And nothing shall deviate Him from
His mission against keeping us apart.
He will suffer greatly and not count
the cost,
For His place is predestined on the
cross.
His death will redefine our life,
For we are now His children, have been
bought at a price.

Jesus Lament's over Jerusalem

Jesus wept because they did not
recognize the time of their visitation
from God.
He wept because now they would no
longer know peace. Their unbelief
would release devastation because
their eyes were closed to the Son of Man
in their midst.

The Cleansing Of The Temple

The house of God, should not be trod
with the money makers and the takers
who would make the house of God
into a den of theives.

The Withered Fig Tree

You are not worthy
         to be alive
         was the reply,
For the fig tree unbarren
could not fulfill its true
life, to sustain the Host
of Heaven in His need.

Judas' Betrayal

Judas', now knew after giving
the thirty pieces of silver
for God's betrayal, and the
kiss that would seal his fate,
was never enough, no amount
would ever be enough for the
ransom of the Son of Man
who is worth more than any
amount that could ever
have been given.

The Last Supper

Seated at the table were the twelve
And Jesus among them did meld
His "Bread of Life" He did held
And the "Blood of Christ" befeld
into the new covenent.

Catherine P. Larsen

The Foot Washing

Bending, washing, showing by deed
The glory of God is to help one in need.

You must show yourselves to be children of light
By serving and loving and being on the side of right.

The Agony In The Garden

Jesus could find nowhere to rest His weary head.
He had come to serve
And His hour had come;
>The hour of agony
>The hour of atonement
>The hour of forgiveness
>The hour of redemption

In the agony in the garden He took the world in His heart and triumphed over evil.

Jesus Promises The Holy Spirit

I must leave so the paraclete will
vivify you and teach and guide you
into all truth.

Peter's Denial

I think Jesus wanted Peter to realize
how easy it could be to deny Him once,
but three times, it reverberated with Peter
like thunder, like brimstone, railing like
lightning-"I don't know this man"-was
a lie an injustice that would be forgiven
because Jesus did know, before the crow,
how Peter's great woe, would help Peter
grow into the rock of the church.

The Crucifiction

Hanging there, why did He not call out His wrath
Against all of the injustices which came to pass?

He could have called His angels to command His wish
To rescue Him from this terrible abyss,

But He didn't
He wouldn't

He would drink the cup
And forever be our Lord and King.

The Resurrection

The light was in Him even in the darkness of the tomb
For no greater love was born of Jesus in His Mother's womb.

Jesus light was stronger than the darkest night.
For three days in the tomb was part of His lonely plight,

To show the world that the world could not contain the King
For Easter Day He rose to bring

The new announcement of His love for us
That hate and death will never conquer LOVE.

www.ingramcontent.com/pod-product-compliance
Lightning Source LLC
Chambersburg PA
CBHW050759160726
48004CB00002B/626